This
Book
Belongs
To _____

Book Club Edition

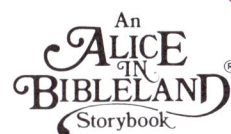

The STORY of ZACCHAEUS

Written by Alice Joyce Davidson
Illustrated by Victoria Marshall

Text copyright © 1997 by Alice Joyce Davidson
Art copyright © 1997 by The C.R. Gibson Company
Published by The C.R. Gibson Company
Norwalk, Connecticut 06856
Printed in the United States of America
All rights reserved.
ISBN 0-7667-1735-6

A little girl named Alice
Had a playhouse in a tree.
She'd often be there reading
With a book propped on her knee.

She had a Bible picture book
With stories told in rhyme,
And Alice loved to read it
When she had some extra time.

One day she read about a man
Who was very, very small,
And how he cheated everyone,
And wasn't liked at all.

The book she held became a screen.
The screen grew tall and wide,
And Alice took a little walk
To Bibleland inside.

Alice went far back in time,
And much to her surprise,
The story of the little man
Came to life before her eyes.

This man was named Zacchaeus.
He lived in Jericho.
He counted lots of money
Making piles all in a row.

He went around collecting tax
From people in the town,
And when he did, they'd greet him
With a most unfriendly frown.

For Zacchaeus was not honest.
He took more than he should,
And he became quite wealthy
Cheating everyone he could.

The people there in Jericho
Stood in the road one day.
They wanted to see Jesus
Who was coming by their way.

Zacchaeus heard the people say
How Jesus loved the poor,
And how God would reward them
For the hardships they endure.

Though this upset Zacchaeus,
Who was a wealthy man,
He decided he'd see Jesus, too,
And hear about God's plan.

He thought, "I see a sycamore.
I'll climb up in that tree.
Then I can look at Jesus,
But he won't see me."

Zacchaeus climbed up in the tree.
The road was right below.
The big leaves covered him so well
He almost didn't show.

Then the crowd became excited,
For coming into view
Were Jesus and His followers,
And His disciples, too.

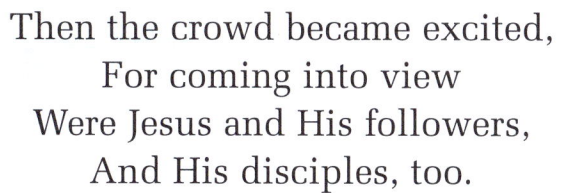

The crowd was quite astonished,
And very puzzled, too,
For visiting a thief
Seemed a strange thing to do.

Zacchaeus, too, was puzzled
As he climbed down from the tree.
But he said to Jesus, "I'd be pleased
If you would dine with me."

Then he felt so awful
That he took more than he should,
He told Jesus he was sorry
And he'd pay back all he could.

Jesus was so happy.
Zacchaeus had changed, it's true.
He said, "God forgives and welcomes you
To serve His Kingdom, too."

The time had come for Alice
To leave that Bible scene.
She came back to her tree house
By walking through her screen.

"I learned a lot," thought Alice
As she climbed down from the tree.
"I learned God's like a father
Who wants the best for me.

"And even when I act real bad,
God will love me still.
He's ready to forgive me
When I have learned His will.

"He's always there to help us change,
and leave our selfish ways,
To truly seek forgiveness,
And follow Him every day.

"When He comes into our lives,
We are renewed once more,
And feel more joy and gladness
Than we ever felt before!"